Holy Communion: Divine Miracle or Simply Symbolic?

By David Stoeckl

Holy Communion: Divine Miracle or Simply Symbolic?

What Does the Bible Teach About the Divine Substance of Communion Bread and Wine?

By David Stoeckl

Published by David Stoeckl and Albedo Books, Sequim, WA 98382
Albedobooks@gmail.com

Cover photo and book design by: David Stoeckl

First printing, April, 2025

ISBN 978-1-967695-11-9 ** Printed Book D2D
ISBN 978-1-967695-08-9 ** ebook D2D

This book is a work of nonfiction in that it is not a fictional novel, but also and more importantly, the Biblical references also make it Historical. Those were real people and real miracles. Some names from my personal accounts and stories may have been changed out of respect to the person, but all miraculous accounts are genuine and authentic. Biblical quotes typically from New International Version Bible.

*** This book composed and produced **without** assistance from **AI**.

To my Mom
who left us this last year
to relocate to the Glory of
Heaven

Miss you, mom

Holy Communion: Divine Miracle or Simply Symbolic?

Introductions and Such

Greetings. Grace and peace to you from God our Father and the Lord Jesus Christ, as St. Paul liked to write.

This little book is actually an expanded part from my book, **Tossing Mountains. Where Are the Miracles Today That We See in the Bible?** This Communion question has been on my heart more and more in recent years, and I believe it would make a very good and quick read for anyone with questions about why and how the Christian Church participates in this holy rite called Communion.

One of the major differences debated throughout the Christian church has been the divine elements of Holy Communion. Does the bread and wine take a divinely transformative change, or is it still just regular, untransformed bread and wine (or juice), eaten in church services merely because Jesus told us to eat in remembrance of Him? This book wishes to focus its considerations regarding the differences in practices of Holy Communion throughout a variety of Christian churches and to seek an honest answer through Holy Scriptures.

We do not go to Holy Communion because we are good; we go to become good.

St. John Bosco

I'm not a major theologian, (or even a Minor Theologian). I just love Christ greatly. That comment is not meant to be a Disclaimer, but more a kind of introduction for me, the author. Most of my books honor Jesus Christ, our LORD and Savior and Messiah. He made it clear to take Communion in remembrance of Him. It's one of the many things Jesus told us to do, and probably holds first place among all other sacraments, including baptism.

Incidentally, in the Gospels Jesus also told us to:
- Repent, continuing with John the Baptist's message as Jesus began His ministry.
- To Not Sin, such as to the woman caught in adultery.
- To Follow Him, His common invitation, starting with His disciples.

6

- To be Baptized, which He told the Apostles to continue doing just before He ascended to Heaven. This includes making disciples – spreading the Word about Jesus so all may believe and be saved.
- To Have Faith and Believe, such as He told Jairus before resurrecting his daughter.
- To Sell all one had and give it to the poor, such as Jesus told the rich, young ruler, for such riches had become a wedge between the young man and the Kingdom of God.
- On the same vein, Jesus told us to *take up one's cross and follow Him.* If we tried to save our lives, we would lose it, but if we gave up our lives for Christ, we would save it.
- To Care for Widows, Orphans and the Poor.
- To Pray for our Enemies, which Jesus stated in Matthew during the Beatitudes. There were no Lead Balloons to go over in 30 A.D., but that teaching would have been a good place for that expression to begin. (How about, "That'll go over like a *lead fig leaf?*")
- To Love the LORD our God with all of our mind, body, soul and strength.
- Similarly, to Love One Another. If you have any questions about your walk with Christ, just check your Agape Love meter.
- From John, my favorite of the four gospels, Jesus told us to Believe that He is in the Father and the Father is in Him. The Father and Jesus are One, B.C., A.D., and Now.D.

7

- To Pray. This is a biggie. Jesus said to Pray Always. Don't pray repetitively like the pagans. Go to the Father in secret – not making a big display on the streets of our prayerfulness. Whatever you do, just keep on praying.
    - The **Our Father**, aka, **The Lord's Prayer**, is a great prayer, declaring our faith in God the Father, asking for our daily bread (yum), and to be delivered as well as give us the wisdom and strength to forgive those who have hurt us. It's an amazing prayer. A dynamo packed prayer.

There are some more thing Jesus said, I'm sure, but you get the idea. Jesus gave us some great directions to live our lives. Notably, Holy Communion is the only one He specifically pronounced to do "in remembrance of" Him. Of course, when we do any of the things Jesus told us to do, as listed above, I expect ALL of them are In Remembrance of Him. Regarding Communion, Jesus wanted BIG focus here. It is not a command to be easily glanced over or get obscured by the list of other to-do's Jesus commanded.

As two pieces of wax fused together make one, so he who receives Holy Communion is so united with Christ that Christ is in him, and he is in Christ.

St. Cyril of Alexandria

Being a person who attended both Catholic and Evangelical Churches over the years, (one denomination at a time =^D), I have been given clear insights into how both viewed and practiced the rites of Communion. Because the belief and practice has such a wide difference theologically, it compelled me to search diligently through Scripture to see what it taught on the subject. If you have similar questions, I pray these will be clearly answered. Many of us have our preconceived beliefs – what others told us to believe about Communion. I tried with all my brain could muster, to set aside those earlier teachings and decide for myself what Scripture clearly said about Communion.

If you disagree with my study, that's between you and God. Same rules apply to me. On the same hand, you're very welcome to show me the errors in my understanding of the Scriptures, but any such arguments mostly need to be under the authority of Holy Scripture. I am not arrogant enough to think for one solitary second, that I fully have the one inroad into the depths and teachings of God's Holy Word.

Another thing I've noticed about this subject is that many already have their beliefs about Holy Communion. Thus, they do not really want their beliefs challenged, including by Holy Scripture. (I call that, "I've already made up my mind. Don't confuse me with the facts.")

Most often, this takes the form of simply NOT addressing Scripture on the subject. Case in point, none of my evangelical friends who have discussed this topic with me want to read this book. We are a stiffnecked people, as God liked to say, where we resist giving up our present beliefs, even if Scripture proves us wrong.

Finally - Enjoy. This study was one of the most blessed and awesome Bible Studies I've ever encountered. I pray you are similarly blessed.

If it is "daily bread," why do you take it once a year? . . . Take daily what is to profit you daily. Live in such a way that you may deserve to receive it daily. He who does not deserve to receive it daily, does not deserve to receive it once a year.

St. Ambrose

Chapter 1 - The Miracle of Holy Communion

There is nothing so great as the Eucharist.
If God had something more precious,
He would have given it to us.

St. John Vianney

There is a common miracle which occurs many, many times each and every day throughout the world. I could not even begin to venture a guess how many times this miracle occurs every day. Jesus established this daily miracle during the Last Supper. The Apostles carried it forward as Jesus instructed, and it is very much practiced right up to this very day. It is the miracle of Holy Communion.

Before I go too far, it would be good to at least list the other sacraments churches practice. Not all churches practice or recognize this list of seven sacraments. Notably, and not so amazing, Holy Communion is the one and only official sacrament practiced in pretty much every Christian Church and Denomination. Even Baptism does not make that list, and Confession, ie, Repenting is something Jesus clearly required, but somehow does not make it as an official Sacrament of all Christian Churches.

The list of Holy Sacraments includes:
- Baptism
- Confession or Penance
- Confirmation
- Matrimony or Marriage
- Holy Orders
- Anointing of the Sick, originally called Extreme Unction, and
- Holy Communion

So, what is Holy Communion? It's the partaking of bread and wine, presented as the body and blood of Jesus Christ, literally eaten by all disciples of Christ, in remembrance of our Lord Jesus.

Here are the Biblical accounts in Matthew, Mark and Luke at the Last Supper, on the evening before Jesus was crucified. The Scriptures are from the NIV, New International Version.

Matthew 26:26-29

While they were eating, Jesus took bread, and when he had given thanks, He broke it and gave it to His disciples, saying, "Take and eat, this is My body."

Then He took the cup, and when He had given thanks, He gave it to them, saying, "Drink from it, all of you. This is my blood of the covenant, which is poured out for many for the forgiveness of sins. I tell you, I will not drink from this fruit of the vine from now on until that day when I drink it new with you in my Father's kingdom."

Mark 14:22-25

While they were eating, Jesus took bread, and when He had given thanks, He broke it and gave it to His disciples, saying, "Take it, this is My body."

Then he took a cup, and when He had given thanks, He gave it to them, and they all drank from it.

"This is My blood of the covenant which is poured out for many," He said to them. "Truly I tell you, I will not drink again from the fruit of the vine until that day when I drink it new in the kingdom of God."

Luke 22:14-20

When the hour came, Jesus and His apostles reclined at the table. And He said to them, "I have eagerly desired to eat this Passover with you before I suffer. For I tell you, I will not eat it again until it finds fulfillment in the kingdom of God."

After taking the cup, He gave thanks and said, "Take this and divide it among you. For I tell you, I will not drink again from the fruit of the vine until the kingdom of God comes."

And He took bread, gave thanks and broke it, and gave it to them, saying, "This is My body given for you; do this in remembrance of Me."

In the same way, after the supper He took the cup, saying, "This cup is the new covenant in My blood, which is poured out for you…"

Jesus completes these verses talking about who would betray Him, seated with them at the Last Supper table.

* **The Gospel of John** does not talk about Holy Communion during the Last Supper like the Coptic Gospels, but has TONS to say about it in Chapter 6 of his Gospel. With that said, John, Chapters 13-17, are his report of the Last Supper. LOTS more shared about what happened that evening, even if St. John did not specifically cover Holy Communion.

In its simplest form, every Christian has the opportunity and ability to consume simple bread and wine as the body and blood of our LORD Jesus Christ. Some Christian sects see this as a miraculous change of substance – that the bread and wine are actually a divine change to the real body and blood of Christ. Many other Christian sects see this as only symbolic and not quite so dynamic a miracle, or no miracle at all.

I recall lessons as a schoolboy where one of my teachers told us that the miracle happened even if we could not see it. It's pretty difficult to explain terms like "substance" to a second grader. She stated that the bread and wine still appeared to be like bread and wine, which was better than eating a raw, bloody bit of meat we were supposed to choke down. That picture stayed with me stronger than most other lessons about communion.

In the Catholic Church, this miracle is called **Transubstantiation**. In Lutheran churches it's called **Consubstantiation**. Anglican/Episcopalian churches don't give it an official name, but over the recent centuries have sided more on the Consubstantiation side. Eastern Orthodox Churches call it the **Mysterion** which is closer if not equal to Transubstantiation.

The difference? For Lutherans, the miraculous change of the bread and wine into the body and blood of Christ only occurs during the church service. Called **Consubstantiation**, which is very different from Transubstantiation, the divine presence of Jesus' body and blood coexist with the common, unremarkable bread and wine. Secondly, after the service is over, the bread and wine are automatically and through no specific words or prayers changed back into natural form so no longer have a holy or divine distinction or substance.

The Catholics believe the **Transubstantiation** of the bread and wine literally becomes the body and blood of Jesus – not just a divine coexistence. It continues to look like bread and wine, but is the adorable, worship-worthy body of our LORD Jesus. They even have a holder, called a ***Monstrance***, to display the consecrated host that may be worshiped. Jesus' body virtually on Earth in the divinely changed bread.

Likewise, Catholics do not put a time limit on the consecrated bread or wine and have a locked case where they keep the consecrated hosts and wine which are not eaten during the service. Oftentimes the priest may consume the rest of the bread and wine during the mass so no consecrated elements will be left.

In the older churches, Catholic, Lutheran, Anglican/Episcopalian and Orthodox, only a licensed minister can perform and distribute Holy Communion.

I have read that Satanists seek the consecrated elements of communion specifically from a Catholic service to desecrate during their coven services. Though that practice is terribly bad, I always wondered that in this way they invited Christ to their services. Christian churches typically do not invite the devil to attend. That partially explains why Catholics teach that only an ordained, Catholic priest, monsignor, bishop, arch-bishop, cardinal or the Pope can consecrate the bread and wine. A nun or monk cannot. The laity cannot consecrate the elements of Holy Communion. If any Catholic could do it, the consecrated hosts and wine could more easily be desecrated, whether intentionally or unintentionally.

As far as I can tell, the Eastern Orthodox Churches **Mysterion** also has no time limit, and the elements of communion remain the body and blood of Christ to be consumed thereafter. Likewise, like the Catholics, only the ordained priests and above can consecrate the bread and wine.

"A thousand years of enjoying human glory is not worth even an hour spent sweetly communing with Jesus in the Blessed Sacrament."
St. Padre Pio

Chapter 2 - Substance or Symbol?

---

*The Holy Eucharist is the perfect expression of
the love of Jesus Christ for man since it is the
quintessence of all the mysteries of His Life.*

St. Peter Julian Eymard

Reared Roman Catholic, I was taught
Transubstantiation. First Communion is a BIG day of
celebration when you're a seven-year-old child in the
Catholic Church. It had been an accepted part of my
Christian life without question until the early 1980's
when I sincerely decided to try to set aside my taught
beliefs and see what Scripture stated. That research
has been resurrected again for this book. I'll give you
exactly what I see in Scripture.

I knew as the protestant churches turned further
away from Catholic Church standards, often seeking a
simpler faith with sincere desire to follow Holy
Scripture, the teaching of Transubstantiation was one
of the first teachings rejected. In turn, many churches
see the bread and wine as simply symbolic of Christ's
body and blood where the real sacrifice happened
some hours later when Jesus was crucified. He died
and three days later resurrected. For them, that's the

real sacrifice which saves us from our sins and begins the New Covenant.

Catholic, Lutheran, Anglican/Episcopalian and Orthodox churches use unleavened bread and wine in their services to follow example similar to what Christ would have used at the Last Supper. As with most things, there are exceptions: the Eastern Catholic Churches use leavened bread and wine. The difference there becomes a historical comparison between the Sacrificial Christ and the Risen Christ.

Many of the Protestant/Evangelical Christian churches, since the Reformation, started to use regular yeast bread or crackers. They also swapped wine for grape juice. Some have communion every single service, and some only occasionally like once a month.

Mormons use regular white bread and water for their communion services, called a Sacrament Meeting.

It's amusing to me to see the pressed, round hosts that are served for communion in many churches. They're hard and tasteless. If you were not careful, it would stick to the roof of your mouth stronger than Neodymium Magnets. They did not come from one loaf like at the Last Supper. The four older churches tell you to <u>not</u> chew the bread with your teeth, but to soften it in your mouth with saliva, then swallow it whole. Many offer a sip of consecrated wine to help. I'm guessing they don't want people leaving church with Jesus' body stuck in their teeth.

Most of the churches which see the elements of communion as symbolic don't care if you chew it or not. Many even dispose of the uneaten elements in the garbage or down the sink, after church – a practice that bothers me a bunch.

I have heard in Hispanic countries, they'll use corn tortillas for communion, though no one has ever officially told me that. I looked up the question on Google and only got tortilla recipes. I found a Jewish website which offered alternatives to wheat products for Passover bread including tortilla chips and rice cakes.

As I considered how to present this miracle for this book, I am very respecting of the variety of Christian churches. Likewise, it would be arrogant to claim I have the one inroad to the truth. I also admit my biases, partially from early life's training, but as I also said, quite some years back I sincerely tried to face this question with Holy Scripture as the only authority and placed that same scrutiny when researching this book. Thus, let me go through Scripture, tell you what I see, and you can decide for yourself whether the practice of Holy Communion is a miraculous change of substance or simply symbolic. Hopefully, you'll keep your mind, heart and spirit as open as I tried to be back then, and still try to be today.

Ask Jesus to make you a Saint. After all,
Only He can do that. Go to Confession regularly
and to Communion as often as you can.

St. Dominic Savio

"This is My Body"

The two statements Christ spoke at the Last Supper,

"This is My body," and *"This is My blood,"*

That seems pretty straightforward to me. Christ didn't say, "This is a representation of My body and blood," or "Eat this bread as My body in My name." Something like that. Jesus held up the bread, broke it and plainly announced, *"This is My body."* Not a lot of gray area in that statement.

He knew He would be physically broken within a few hours. The bread does have a strong and deeply motivating symbolism when considered that Christ held up the bread to his disciples like a visual aid. He ripped it apart using His own hands as He told them, *"This is My body."*

The wine Jesus did not rip-up, destroy, or pour out. Instead, the wine became the declaration of His New Covenant. All three Synoptic Gospels use the word, "**Covenant**" with the wine, but only Luke calls it a "**New Covenant**".

What a difference it would have been to us if the gospel authors all stated, "He took the cup and poured it out on the floor, in the same fashion as Christ's blood was poured out as He was beaten, scourged and crucified." But that didn't happen. Like the bread, they were all to consume it, all drinking from the same goblet.

One word really stands out to me in both of those pronouncements. The word is small, so often gets overlooked. The word is "IS". In English it is a "To Be" verb, present tense. It is a word of being. An absolute. Jesus said, "This IS my body." It's His body NOW – not tomorrow or a few days later after He resurrects. His body and blood are in the bread and wine right there at the Last Supper.

I do not know much ancient Greek, Hebrew or Aramaic – the languages the Bible was originally written. I cannot conjugate one verb for you in any of those three languages. Still, if I understand correctly, the To Be verb IS does not exist in Aramaic. It does exist in ancient Hebrew and Greek. Thus, the translation is not incorrect or grammatically strained. English alliteration and syntax requires use of such verbs, whether present tense like IS, or past tense like WAS, or future tense like WILL BE.

In turn, Jesus did not say, "This WAS My Body," or "This WILL BE My Body."

I have no reason to believe the twenty centuries that Holy Scripture has been studied with the utmost of care, seeking God's absolute truths by truly devout men and women, (including the last few centuries since

21

it has been translated into English, German, etc.), yet no one with scholarly Biblical authority claims that the present tense "This *IS* My Body" was translated improperly for Jesus at the Last Supper in any of those three gospels. Jesus equated the bread and wine as His body and blood right there and then.

Receive Communion often, very often . . . there you have the sole remedy, if you want to be cured. Jesus has not put this attraction in your heart for nothing.

St. Therese of Lisieux

Chapter 3 - The New Covenant Established During the Last Supper?

I may be wrong in my understanding to state that one major reason many Protestant faiths reject a substantial change of the bread and wine is because it could thereby be argued that the bread and wine solely and totally created and established the new covenant. If so, then Jesus would not have had to die or resurrect. That ideology completely rubs against the fact that Christ's sacrifice on the cross wiped away all sins, not the Lord's Supper. There's more than enough Scripture that points to Jesus' prophesied crucifixion as the Pascal sacrifice for our sins, made complete by His resurrection and ascension.

Still, that begs the question why Jesus would firmly state,

"This cup is the New Covenant in My blood…"

if the sacrifice was not complete until Calvary? Did the New Covenant begin at the Last Supper? Jesus seems to say it does.

My best answer, and I welcome others to share their insights, is that both the Last Supper and the Crucifixion are part of the same redeeming string of activities. Like the Crucifixion led to the Resurrection led to the Ascension led to the descent of the Holy Spirit, the Lord's Supper could have been a crucial part – even the starting point for the New Covenant. That could further explain why Jesus put so much emphasis on remembering Him through Communion.

There's a communion of more than our bodies when bread is broken and wine drunk.

M. F. K. Fisher

For that matter, the sacrificial death and resurrection of Jesus goes back to His birth, and even centuries before when His virgin birth was prophesied. He had to be born with a human body to be the sacrificial lamb on Calvary. It's not hard to see how His few years of ministry led up to the crucifixion. That same three years also led to the Lord's Supper as part of God's loving plans for our salvation.

A second answer to Jesus saying the wine was His blood for the New Covenant goes a bit more ethereal. We are linear creatures. In this life we are typically stuck in time and space. Spiritual bodies are not. God created time and space. Time and space did not exist before God.

To disagree that the New Covenant in Christ's blood began with the elements of communion at the Last Supper is to claim Jesus lied, or at least His words were not reported accurately in those three gospels. Lots of loosened, canned worms if you believe those alternative arguments. For Jesus at the Last Supper to recognize the New Covenant creates changes in the Heavenly Realm outside time and space. Timeless and spaceless, Jesus' words equally connect to the

24

effects of His crucifixion which would be the same non-time and space as His Resurrection, etc. in God's Heavenly realm.

Holy Communion is the shortest
And safest way to Heaven.

Pope Pius X

Perhaps more simply put, in the Heavenly realm, the Last Supper, crucifixion, resurrection and ascension occurred as one singular activity, like the different acts of the same stage play. Jesus as our Creator God does not have to follow the plodding motions of time and space that took Him to the cross the next day to make all complete. He did not hang out in the grave three linearly measured days for His benefit, but for our benefit and the fulfillment of prophetic Scripture.

Now here is what the Apostle Paul wrote about Holy Communion.

I Cor. 11:23-28

(The Apostle Paul wrote): For I received from the Lord what I also passed on to you: The Lord Jesus on the night he was betrayed, took bread,

and when He had given thanks, He broke it and said, "This is my body, which is for you; do this in remembrance of Me."

In the same way, after supper He took the cup, saying, "This cup is the new covenant in My blood; do this whenever you drink it, in remembrance of Me." For whenever you eat this bread and drink this cup, you proclaim the Lord's death until He comes.

So then, whoever eats the bread or drinks the cup of the Lord in an unworthy manner will be guilty of sinning against the body and blood of the Lord. Everyone ought to examine themselves before they eat of the bread and drink from the cup.

In this part of St. Paul's first letter to the Corinthian Church, he has just scolded them for basically partying at church. Reportedly, some were eating and drinking, including getting drunk, before others arrived. In verses 20-21, Paul wrote,

"So then, when you come together, it is not the Lord's Supper you eat, for when you are eating, some of you go ahead with your own private suppers. As a result, one person remains hungry and another gets drunk."

He started by correcting a perversion of communion by the Corinthian Church. Next, Paul explained to them again what communion was about – the part quoted above.

We know that St. Paul was not present at the Last Supper. This Apostle, called in a very direct and dramatic manner by Jesus Christ, was surely told about communion by one of the Apostles after his conversion. I'm guessing it was Peter who brought a potential persecutor to the Christian believers in Jerusalem. They spent fifteen days together in Jerusalem some years after Paul's call and conversion. Yet, Paul stated in verse 23,

"*For I received from the Lord* *what I also passed on to you.*"

Paul was claiming the authority of his letter came directly from the words of Jesus Christ, God Almighty, spoken directly to His servant and son Paul, specifically regarding this subject.

The word *"received,"* past tense. The Lord has already given these words to him.

The Eucharist is the source and
summit of the Christian life.

Pope John Paul II

His account over the next two verses are very similar to the three Synoptic Gospel accounts.

   – *"This is My body."* *"This cup is the <u>new</u> covenant in My blood."* *"...Do this in remembrance of Me,"* (Jesus).

   Then, Paul's next words explain part of the beauty of the sacrament of Communion beyond what the three gospel writers wrote.

   "For whenever you eat this bread and drink this cup, you proclaim the Lord's death until He comes."

   We Christians proclaim the Lord's death until He comes. Over and over, Scripture points to the ultimate sacrifice of the Paschal Lamb, Jesus, sinless yet condemned to death on a cross for our sins. Holy Communion makes a statement – a proclamation. To partake of the bread and wine is to be a herald to all people, that Christ died for all of us. That statement also could support my consideration that the New Covenant began with the Last Supper Communion, connecting it with the crucifixion sacrifice, bodily resurrection, ascension and descent of the Holy Spirit.

   If you continued to read Paul's account in First Corinthians 11, Paul told them that many of their maladies and weaknesses and even deaths had come from not paying homage and reverence to the Lord's Supper. This is not small stuff.

Paul wrote in I Cor. 11:27

"So then, whoever eats the bread or drinks the cup of the Lord in an unworthy manner will be guilty of <u>sinning against the body and blood</u> of the Lord."

It seems to me a stretch to say anyone could be guilty of sinning against some unaltered, simply symbolic, not consecrated bread and wine, eaten in the name of the Lord.

Paul's words strike me as some pretty divinely powerful bread and wine. I am in awe of those words. In this passage, Paul did not claim that we sin against God or the Spirit of God or the Holy Spirit or the Ten Commandments. He wrote that we sin against <u>the body and blood of Christ</u>.

A couple verses later, Paul wrote,

"For those who eat and drink without discerning the body of Christ, eat and drink judgment on themselves. That is why many among you are weak and sick, and a number of you have fallen asleep."

Paul specifically instructed the Corinthian Church, (and us), to *discern the Body of Christ*. That is to ponder on it to full understanding. To discern the Body of Christ, we must not take Holy Communion in an unworthy manner. To fail here is to <u>eat and drink judgment upon oneself</u>. That makes for some pretty potently valued bread and wine to avoid eating and drinking judgment upon ourselves.

This made it kind of a no-brainer for me. It's easy to understand, if we do not discern and follow Christ, we condemn ourselves. We bring God's judgment upon ourselves. Here, Paul places that same urgency upon these simple elements of bread and wine that Jesus told us to eat in remembrance of Him.

As you know, St. Paul came from a Jewish background. The Jews had LOTS of food limitations. Mosaic Law made it a sin to eat those forbidden foods. When you think about it, even Adam and Eve in the garden had food limitations. Foods consecrated for the priests would also be a sin for most to eat.

Young not-yet-King David was the one example of not sinning eating such bread. Still, St. Paul realigns Jewish practice by discerning and considering the Body of Christ in the bread and wine. Short of this, we bring judgment upon ourselves when we merely consume without discerning, (ie, fully recognizing) the elements of Holy Communion.

Answer this question for yourself: can a person sin against bread and wine as a mere symbol of Christ's presence in the elements of communion, or would Christ have to be truly present in the substance of bread and wine for humans to sin against it?

When you look at the Sacred Host, you understand how much Jesus loves you now.

Mother Teresa

Chapter 4 - John 6:25-71

This lengthy part of the Gospel of John has been called **The Discourse on the Bread of Life**. It's also called **Jesus, the Bread of Life**.

I believe St. John wrote this part of his gospel to specifically testify to what Jesus said about Holy Communion. The other three Gospels had already been written. John certainly knew about them. He covered many items the other three did not, including the wedding feast in Cana and the resurrection of Lazarus. I cannot help but think that he wrote this in light of opposition and controversies in the early Christian Church that opposed the divine miracle of Holy Communion. Best of all, he a firsthand witness, reported it in Jesus' own words.

Jesus has just miraculously fed over 5,000 people with bread and fish. Then, He walked upon the Sea of Galilee at night, passing the Apostles in a boat during a storm. Next Simon Peter walked on the water with Jesus, for a short time before sinking and returning to the surface by Jesus' hand. Next, Jesus calmed the storm when He got into the boat. Suddenly, they were near shore.

Arriving in or near Capernaum on the north coast of the Sea of Galilee, a large crowd sought Jesus. Many of them had dined on miraculously multiplied cuisine the day or two before. Jesus addressed their simple and understandable motives to be fed again, then took it somewhat deeper telling them to seek Spiritual food that does not spoil. In that way, the feeding 5,000 became a setup for Jesus' discourse.

The crowd asked a very good question:

"What must we do to do the works God requires?"

The answers to this question had been part of their lives and culture under the Ten Commandments and Mosaic Law since before any of them were born, yet they asked Jesus what they must do.
I loved His answer.

"The work of God is this to believe in the One He has sent."

We didn't have to "work" at all; only to <u>believe</u>.

I am always puzzled by those in the Bible who encounter some super-duper amazing miracle of God that they somehow shove behind them like it didn't happen and ask for another sign from Heaven. ("That was then. This is now, LORD.") The Israelites did it big time to Moses, including Heaven-sent food for them to collect each and every day; more than enough to feed an army. St. John wrote that those talking to Jesus in Capernaum mentioned manna. Jesus had just fed the five thousand. God fed the Israelites manna in the wilderness. It was no accident both of those miracles were brought together for this discourse.

On the other hand, apparently not all there questioning Jesus came across the Sea of Galilee, following Him to get more bread and fish. The west coast towns of Gennesaret and Tiberius are both mentioned in various Gospels, bringing their sick, even carried on mats, for Jesus to heal. All wound-up in Capernaum.

Sidenote: besides the woman who had an issue of blood for twelve years healed when she touched Jesus' clothing, many in this account in the Gospel of Mark were also healed by just a touch of Jesus' clothes.

Have a great love for Jesus in His Divine Sacrament of Love; that is the Divine Oasis of the Desert. It is the Heavenly Manna of the traveler. It is the Holy Ark. It is the Life and Paradise of Love on Earth.

St. Peter Julian Eymard

Returning to John, Chapter 6, Jesus then reminded them that Moses did not do anything – God the Father supplied the manna. Jesus pointed them right to the source of their lives. Then, Jesus went past manna to introduce them to the *"true bread from Heaven."* It seems to me more likely that Jesus' words were taken metaphorically here, as He first called Himself bread, and implied that manna only fed Moses and the Israelites, whereas this bread of God *"comes down from Heaven and gives life to the world."*

Very reasonably, they said,

"Sir, always give us this bread."

Who wouldn't want bread from Heaven which gives life to the world? Did they realize that Jesus was not talking about something like the return of manna, or Jesus multiplying loaves of bread every day? Probably not at this point.

Thus, Jesus replied with additional information to what He had just told them. You want this bread? Good news. He's standing right in front of you.

Jesus declared, *"I am the bread of life. Whoever comes to Me will never go hungry, and whoever believes in me will never be thirsty."*

He's just told them that the source of this bread is Heaven. He's just told them that this bread gives life to the whole entire world. Now Jesus added that He is that very bread they just told Him that they wanted every day. He also said they would never go "thirsty". Bread doesn't usually quench one's thirst, so we have a teaching which perhaps correlates with bread as a metaphoric liquid to also quench the thirst of those who seek God.

Two other gospel Scriptures come to mind for me. The first is Luke 4:16-20 where Jesus was in the synagogue where they asked him to read from Isaiah about the Messiah. Jesus read the passage, sat down a moment, then He added,

"Today this Scripture is fulfilled in your hearing."

Here in John 6:35, Jesus made a similar Messianic reference about Himself to the crowd in Capernaum, claiming He came down from Heaven.

Jesus has made Himself the Bread of Life to give us life. Night and day, He is there. If you really want to grow in love, come back to the Eucharist; come back to that Adoration.

Mother Teresa

The second Scripture which came to mind was John, Chapter 4, where Jesus passed through Samaria with His Apostles. They stopped to rest by Jacob's Well in Sychar. A lone woman came by to draw water. Jesus asked her for a drink, opening the door to a wonderful conversation about living water – water that one may drink and never again thirst. Like the woman who wanted living water so she would never again thirst, the crowd at Capernaum wanted Bread of Life so they would never again hunger.

Jesus continued to tell them about Himself, coming down from Heaven for all of them, calling Himself the Bread of Life and He was the Living Bread.

Their reaction? Oddly, they ignored everything else He said and focused on, "Hey! Wait a minute. You're the carpenter's son. We know your family. You didn't come down on some cloud from Heaven. You cannot be anyone sent directly from God. I'm paraphrasing here, of course. You get the gist. They ignored the real message, stumbled by the simple fact that Jesus, who's earthly, human birth and life were prophesied, especially in Isaiah, was well, actually born and grew-up like the Old Testament prophets foretold. For whatever reason, they're all ignoring Old Testament prophesies while looking at Jesus and thinking, "That can't be right. He grew-up around here."

John's account does not tell us, but I'm expecting some of the Capernaum locals had joined the group who crossed the Sea of Galilee since they knew he was a local boy. For that matter, it wouldn't take more than one or two Capernaum-ites to identify Jesus' hometown, but I'm expecting Jesus addressed more than just a few here. Eventually, they would wind up in the Capernaum synagogue, so much of the town would be there to see Jesus.

Until we have a passionate love for our Lord
In the Most Blessed Sacrament,
We shall accomplish nothing.

St. Peter Julian Eymard

Keith Green

One of my favorite Christian musical performers is Keith Green who died in July, 1982. In *Song to My Parents*, he sang,

"Isn't that Jesus? Isn't that Joseph and Mary's son? Well, didn't He grow-up right here? He played with our children. What! He must be kidding. Thinks He's a prophet. Well, prophets don't grow-up from little boys. Do they? From little boys? Do they?"

Jesus told them He would bring them to eternal life and raise them up on the last day. Talk about BIG WOW statements. Yet, all they could see was one of their own who grew up about twenty-five miles away, there in Galilee. He fed them and walked on water and a whole bunch of other miracles and healing, plus wise words and teachings, but somehow those didn't weigh as heavily to the crowd as the fact that Jesus grew-up in a little town in Galilee.

Jesus rebuked their narrow-sighted rejection of Him and continued to teach. He was from God. He had seen the Father. He repeated that He was the Bread of Life. Your ancestors ate manna and still died. Receive Jesus as the Bread of Life and not die. He is Living Bread which came down from Heaven. Whoever ate that Living Bread would live forever.

Then, His next sentence probably made more than a few heads turn. He said,

"This bread is my flesh, which I will give for the life of the world."

A couple thousand years later, we're reading this and thinking, "He's talking about the Last Supper. He's talking about His sacrifice on the cross. He gave Himself fully for the life of the world." That would not be an unreasonable reading, but that's not what the crowd heard. The Last Supper, Crucifixion and Resurrection are still a ways off in their futures.

They argued sharply amongst themselves,

"How can this man give us His flesh to eat?"

There are times when we read in Scripture a response to something Jesus, (and others) said, and you know those listening got it wrong. That's not the case here.

It's like John 10:30 when Jesus said,

"The Father and I are One."

The Jewish leaders didn't say, "Oh, He means one in purpose." No, they recognized that Jesus meant He was on equal footing with God their Father. In response, they picked up stones to execute Jesus for His "blasphemy". It never occurred to them even once that Jesus' words could have actually been the truth.

"The Holy Eucharist is the perfect expression of the love of Jesus Christ for man."
St. Maria Goretti

In Capernaum, the crowd totally recognized that Jesus was talking about His physical flesh being the Bread of Life. The idea was clearly repulsive to those hearing Jesus.

And notice that Jesus didn't say, "Wait! No, no, no. You misunderstood. That's not what I meant at all. Uh-uh." Jesus didn't stutter. Instead, He continued along that same teaching.

"*Very truly*," He began, stressing the authenticity of His words, *"I tell you, unless you <u>eat the flesh of the Son of Man and drink His blood</u>, you have no life in you. <u>Whoever eats my flesh and drinks my blood has eternal life</u>, and I will raise them up at the last day."*

We don't get audience reaction here. I'm guessing many were too stunned to say anything. The picture of gnawing on Jesus gnarly hide would not be a welcome picture in their minds. This is first century Israel under Roman occupation. They haven't seen Silence of the Lambs, or traveled Donner's Pass by horse drawn wagon, but they had seen greater atrocities by their Roman captors. Similarly, cannibalism was considered the lowest of the low in Scripture. The Old Testament citations mostly address eating your offspring. **Micah 3:2-3** clearly calls cannibalism an atrocity. It's always, always one of the worst things a person can do.

In like manner, God set us apart from all other life on earth. We were not to sacrifice each other on an altar for sins nor any other reason. Our lives are a special gift. Refraining from cannibalism is not a direct command from God in Scripture; not one of the Ten

Commandments, but still not a stretch to say that Scripture clearly indicated, "Thou shalt not eat each other."

So, Jesus directing them to eat His flesh and drink His blood was very, very repulsive to the crowd in Capernaum.

We're not talking about the Jewish religious leaders in Jerusalem getting their tunics all in a wad, though somewhere along the way Jesus left the beach to give this lesson in the Capernaum synagogue, (verse 59). Verse 52 says the Jews began to argue sharply among themselves... Rabbis were surely there, but none are specifically recorded. Doesn't matter. Cannibalism in Judea and Galilee was never ever considered okay.

Communion is as necessary for us to sustain our Christian vitality, as the vision of God is necessary to the angels, to maintain their life of glory.

St. Peter Julian Eymard

I recently heard a blessed pastor who lives in Colorado talk about I Corinthians 11. His main argument against the bread and wine turned into the Body and Blood of Jesus was that it would be like cannibalism. I would agree with him if Jesus had not *made that point very and completely clear that was exactly what He was instructing.* Cannibalism was not okay, but in the New Covenant, Jesus suggesting a cannibalistic observance was somehow still to be practiced. I expect eating divinely transformed bread and wine is Not the same cannibalistic practice as eating the flesh of a human being intrinsically because it is divine.

Many folks acknowledge that we receive God's Holy Spirit in a wide variety of manners and methods, but they still draw the line at virtually eating Jesus flesh and blood.

Similarly, it trips some people out to think that Jesus had Jesus in His own hands as He ripped apart the bread at The Last Supper, and told His Apostles to eat. Personally, that doesn't bother me any more than biting my fingernails or some shards of dead skin on my hands, or biting my tongue or cheek or lip. In obedience to the Father, Jesus intentionally gave His body to be broken and ripped apart that very night. In my limited understanding, Jesus ripping apart the bread that He had just declared was His Body is no more painful or weird than any of us eating that bread and drinking that wine during Communion.

Recognize this bread what hung on the cross, and in this chalice what flowed from His side. . .

whatever was in many and varied ways announced beforehand in the sacrifices of the Old Testament pertains to this one sacrifice which is revealed in the New Testament.

St. Augustine

My Flesh is Real Food and My Blood is Real Drink

Next, as if He had not confounded them enough already, Jesus made eating His flesh and drinking His blood <u>mandatory</u>. If you didn't eat it, you would have <u>no life</u> in you. But munch on His carcass and you'll have eternal life in you and will be raised up on the last day.

Again, no response as yet from the crowds in the synagogue.

At this point, as weird as this teaching may have seemed, it could have still been perhaps considered metaphoric. Allegorical. Poetic imagery, even with the crowd's reactions. Then, verses 55 to 58 turned-over that picture to create a totally new light shed on the subject.

Jesus said,

"For my flesh is <u>real food</u> and my blood is <u>real drink</u>. Whoever eats my flesh and drinks my blood remains in me, and I in them. Just as the living Father sent me and I live because of the Father, so the one who feeds on me will live because of Me. This is the bread that came down from Heaven. Your ancestors ate manna and died, but whoever feeds on this bread will live forever."

Jesus' flesh is real food and His blood is real drink. That idea just went from colorful imagery to hard fact. This went beyond the Samaritan woman at the well wanting living water. Jesus never claimed His living water was real drink. It remained in the Spiritual realm for our souls to consume. Here He clearly declared His flesh and blood to be real food, just as real as the manna the Israelites ate in the desert.

How did the crowd react? They were weirded-out. They choked.

"This is a hard teaching. Who can accept it?"

Here St. John changed focus a bit. Before Jesus was speaking to the crowd in the synagogue. Now some of His own <u>disciples</u> began grumbling about this teaching.

I cannot even blame them. I'd be furrowing brows as well, saying something like, "Jesus, You said, 'Repent,' and I repented. You said, 'Be baptized,' so I did that, too. You turned water into wine, and You sent a bunch of us out to heal the sick and expel demons in Your name. You healed a royal official's son, and a man paralyzed for thirty-eight years. You miraculously fed thousands of us and walked on water. I can totally see how God is with You, but this latest teaching, to instruct us to eat Your flesh and drink Your blood, and if we don't, we have no share in God's kingdom with You seems pretty bizarre for me to wrap my head around."

Jesus knew the oddity of this teaching. In turn, it was perfect that Jesus did not ignore their concerns. He asked them directly,

"Does this offend you?"

He already knew the answer, so continued, asking,

"Then what if you see the Son of Man ascend to where He was before? The Spirit gives life; the flesh counts for nothing. The words I have spoken to you — they are full of the Spirit and life. Yet there are some of you who do not believe."

I love this. He moved into the prophetic, or more exactly, responded by showing them a little of His future events, already planned-out and put into motion. He asked them what they would do after He returned to the Father (Ascension) and sent the Holy Spirit to give us His abundant life more fully. Thus, our flesh counts for nothing. Our corporeal selves and physical world are mere coverings of our real selves. Our clothing. Our costumes and masks. The real, eternal us cannot be seen by human eyes or felt by fingers, yet that part of each of us is more real than anything we see or are while alive on this planet. And, That substantiates Jesus' words, ***"full of the Spirit and life."***

He said some of them would not believe, then St. John wrote that Jesus always knew who would believe and who would not. John probably saw this ability of Jesus in action over and over and over from John's front row seat as an Apostle.

Jesus' next words were very special to behold. Don't glaze your eyes as you glance over them. They are worth a special, very close look and scrutiny. He said,

"*This is why I told you that no one can come to Me unless the Father has enabled him.*"

Think about that verse for a moment before you continue reading.

For some pages Jesus has been saying things like:
- "*No one comes to the Father except by Me.*" – John 14:6
- "*No one has seen the Father except the one who is from God; only He has seen the Father.*" – John 6:46
- "*No one has ever seen God, but the one and only Son, who is Himself God and is in closest relationship with the Father, has made Him known.*" – John 1:18

This time, Jesus seemed to say the exact opposite. They could not come to Jesus except when the Father enabled them. This is one of those moments sharing how Jesus and the Father really are One. Jesus is Creator just as the Father is Creator, (and so is the Holy Spirt, by the way, but I may save that for another book or blog or newsletter). Now we cannot even come to Jesus unless we are enabled by The Father to seek and be with Jesus. It's almost like double talk from John 14:6. *No one comes to the Father except by Me, oh and by the way, no one comes to Me except by the Father.* That would be a closed loop for us humans, but Jesus would have no problem making it happen for all of us.

Jesus even repeated that same teaching in verse 6:44.

No one can come to Me unless the Father who sent Me draws them, and I will raise them up on the last day.

This fits in with Jesus' words that no one comes to Father except through Him. That He is the only way to the Father. (John 14:6). There are other Scriptures that verify Jesus is the only way to God. God directs us to Jesus who raises us up on the last day to God the Father.

In its simplest terms, Jesus and God the Father are ever and always One. Mostly, Jesus speaks of His relationship with the Father, but even the Holy Spirit is present in 6:63.

The Spirit gives life; the flesh counts for nothing…

Jesus reminds them the Holy Spirit is also present as they question and even start to move away from Jesus over this teaching.

It's also a special instruction of His divine authority – a road map for those there, even if they were still having trouble with this 'eat Your flesh and drink Your blood' teaching. Jesus showed them the door and gave them the key. They didn't even have to wipe their feet before entering. The Spirit of Almighty God has always been with Israel. This was still totally true while Jesus of Nazareth walked the earth, even as it is today. In like manner, Jesus told them to seek the Father, and His words really would literally become saving grace for them.

…In this world, I cannot see
the Most High Son of God with my own eyes,
except for His Most Holy Body and Blood.
St. Francis of Assisi

When I am confounded by the words of Jesus, and there were some really perplexing things He said, I can now look-up commentaries on the internet and read the books of other men and women more blessed and knowledgeable than myself. In turn, all wisdom and knowledge I could acquire needs still be brought home in my mind, heart, body, soul and spirit when the fullness of God personally fills me to overflowing. Sitting here, typing this, I am getting more and more giddy just thinking about it and remembering those special moments. I mention this to report to you that I also referred to the wisdom of others to compose this book.

Now, before you think I've gone way off subject on some crazy tangent which didn't answer the question by which this book is based, this chapter in John was perhaps the most revealing over any others in the Bible about communion.

Verse 6:66 says, *"From that time many of his disciples turned back and no longer followed Him."*

If Jesus didn't say something totally upsetting to the crowd, they would not have rejected Him at this time. They definitely understood His words – that they were to literally eat His flesh and drink His blood, and that His flesh and blood were real food. Their rejection absolutely validates how they fully understood Jesus' words.

Also, you know it was no accident when whoever made up the chapters and verses for the Scriptures intentionally made this one to have three sixes, like the Mark of the Beast in the Book of Revelation. It's virtually the only place in all of the New Testament with a chapter 6, verse 66.

By the way, the Old Testament also has one:

I Chronicles 6:66 *Some of the Kohathite clans were given as their territory towns from the tribe of Ephraim.*

Doesn't quite have the same damning bite as John 6:66.

The notable point for this book is that the meanings behind Jesus' words about eating His flesh and drinking His blood were completely understood and rejected by even some of His disciples. It would not be until at the Last Supper, just before Jesus died, that those words would be brought to understandable application for us.

This supernatural bread and this consecrated chalice are for the health and salvation of mankind.

St. Cyprian

Looking at the small picture as we humans so often do, myself included, how could everyone in all the earth from Jesus to now and beyond possibly eat Jesus' flesh and drink His blood? Besides the fact that His human body no longer exists on the Earth since He ascended, He used only a single human body - not nearly enough of His physical body for every one of His disciples to eat any significant amount with any regularity.

"This is your single cell of Jesus' flesh and single cell of blood. We have to make sure there's enough to go around until Jesus returns."

Nope. It didn't work like that, and God never intended it that way. Over a year later, in an upper room celebrating the most significant holy occasion of the Jewish year, Jesus and his twelve closest associates shared the Passover meal, also called the Feast of Unleavened Bread. It was there that His body became real food and His blood real drink.

I wish I'd been there to see Him take the bread and break it, give it to all His Apostles and declare to them an answer they may never have had answered before that moment. *"THIS IS MY BODY."*

Jesus never said to Himself, "I will probably die tomorrow. Are there any loose ends? Oh, yeah. That *'eat My body and drink My blood'* teaching I did up in Capernaum. Went over like a lead balloon, (lead fig leaf?). I still hear criticisms about it through the grapevine. Maybe I should explain it better. A little damage control before I depart this life. Hey! There's bread and wine here. I'll use these for visual aids and go to the cross without that misinterpretation following Me to My grave."

No, Jesus didn't say anything like that. When He said, *"This is My Body,"* He totally foreknew the application and correlations to Him being the Bread of Life.

"Ohhhhhh," some of His apostles may have thought. "THAT'S what He meant. We never could figure that out. Back in Capernaum, we said that we'd still stay with Him, and that we did. We saw so many amazing things – people raised from the dead, demons expelled, people healed even of infirmities from birth, issues of blood stopped; even wind and wave obeying His very words as well as His amazing teachings plus standing up to and even silencing the Jewish leaders, but we never could figure out what He meant by *'My flesh is real food and My blood is real drink.'* The light finally dawns, and we understand for the first time."

Or, perhaps Jesus explained it to them before they went to bed that night back in Chapter 6 Capernaum. No way to know before we depart this life.

What is important is that Jesus intentionally did not show them the miraculous gift of Holy Communion with the bread and wine as the body and blood of Jesus in Capernaum, or anywhere else before the Last Supper. That time had not yet come. Yet, at the Last Supper, Jesus must have stressed the importance of Communion more than Scripture even relays to us, for it has become the mainstay in the Christian churches, grounded by the Apostles and continued through the Apostolic Fathers, to be practiced throughout the centuries.

Consider how confusing it would have been for the Apostles if Jesus did Holy Communion multiple times - like each week before He was arrested and crucified. *("Hey guys, I know I'm still here, but I need you to eat my flesh and drink my blood, again. I really want you to get this one right").*

Instead, Jesus used the one Passover Meal before His arrest. He stressed for His disciples to do this in remembrance of Him. In that, we the church continue to be obedient as we partake of the holy elements of Communion.

The four older churches tell you to Not chew the bread with your teeth, but to soften it in your mouth with saliva, then swallow it whole. Many offer a sip of consecrated wine to help. I'm guessing they don't want people leaving church with Jesus' body stuck in their teeth.

David Stoeckl

One More (Kinda BIG) Thought

It's regarding celebrating Holy Communion in Remembrance of Jesus, and the New Covenant.

Consider why would Jesus tell us to partake of Holy Communion in Remembrance of Him? Does that one-of-a-kind command of our Lord suggest a special significance or importance to Holy Communion?

I expect most would say, "Yes."

Just for the record, Matthew and Mark do not include the Remembrance line. Luke quotes Jesus be remembered regarding only the bread, and Paul in First Corinthians cites "Do this in remembrance of Me," for both the bread and the wine.

Re-editing this book, I heard the Lord say to me the word, "Bridge."

By His Word I considered, Holy Communion takes two simple products of this world, consecrates them and makes them holy and divine. If the bread and wine truly become the Body and Blood of Christ, they become a **literal, virtual BRIDGE between Heaven and Earth; ie, a very real Connection between God and His creation.** We who are corruptible sinners can literally receive the sinless eternal body and blood of the risen Christ Jesus into our bodies. **Could it be that Connection, that Bridge, establishes the actual foundation to begin Jesus Christ's New Covenant that He announced at the Last Supper?**

We are all acutely aware that our lives on this side of the grave are temporary. Jesus clearly said our souls will live-on, even forever, after we shed these corruptible tents of flesh and blood. Scripture is clear that Jesus totally defeated death. To partake of His living Body and Blood potentially connects that bridge between Heaven and our short lives on Earth.

I cannot think of a better reason why Jesus would want us to Remember Him this way. Connecting in that specific and physical way, Christ's divine presence makes Holy Communion all the more vitally important for our Earthly lives with Father God.

Consequently, it seems to me that no simply symbolic bread or wine (or juice) could establish such a holy, miraculous bridge or connection between God and His creation. Neither could it establish Christ's New Covenant. As is, simply symbolic bread and wine offer little to no valid or holy consecration for it to be remembered or practiced.

Chapter 5 - The Road to Emmaus

This is one of those things that needs to be added. In Luke 24, two disciples of Christ, not previously named in Scripture, (one named Cleopas), were walking after Jesus died, to the town of Emmaus. Emmaus is roughly seven miles east by northeast of Jerusalem.

The two men are joined by Jesus, but they didn't recognize Him. (I wonder if Jesus still had the holes in his hands and feet for them to see?) He walked with them, explaining Old Testament prophesies that pointed to Him being Messiah. Personally, I wish Luke had been more specific to list some of those prophesies, (even if I can do a quick Google search and get in seconds the list of the over 300 Old Testament prophesies that Jesus fulfilled.)

The men reached Emmaus and invited Jesus to lodge with them. They sat down to eat, and Jesus commenced a Holy Communion service.

Luke 24:30 – *When He was at the table with them, He took bread, gave thanks, broke it and began to give it to them. Then their eyes were opened and they recognized Him, and He disappeared from their sight.*

This is a very nice verification that Jesus meant for us to practice Holy Communion even after He resurrected.

Finally, there are at least two other brief mentions of Holy Communion in the Book of Acts.

Acts 2:42 - *And they devoted themselves to the apostles' teaching and the fellowship, to the <u>breaking of bread</u> and the prayers.*

Acts 20:7 - *On the first day of the week, when we were gathered together to <u>break bread</u>, Paul talked with them, intending to depart on the next day, and he prolonged his speech until midnight.*

These are also worth mentioning in that the Apostles and Disciples of Christ continued to practice Holy Communion even after Jesus' Ascension into Heaven.

So, are they symbolic or a true transformation in substance? That is only a question you can answer for yourself. I have a few more thoughts on that subject.

The first is that regardless what you may think of the **Roman Catholic Church**, that is the church which directly came forth from Jesus and the Apostles who carried the torch of Christ's love and message to the world. There are some really awesome and devout Christians who think the Catholic Church is the anti-Christ. I encounter them regularly. Very sad, especially because there's already too much anti-Christian evil in the world. How can we so harshly judge some very beautiful and loving people who believe the same core values of Christian faith, seek to serve God and live lives in the Spirit of Christ?

In turn, my main point here is that those Christians who so vigorously oppose the Catholic Church claim <u>Scriptural Authority</u> for their judgments against the Catholic Church. Yet it is those very Scriptures that God gave the Catholic Church to both compile the twenty-seven books, then maintain its integrity for over a millennium. By God's Word and decision, we have the Holy Scriptures today because of the Roman Catholics. Even the Orthodox Churches use the same canonical Scriptures as the Catholic Church, plus they added four more Old Testament Sections:

- 3 & 4 Maccabees
- Psalm 151
- The Prayer of Manasseh in Chronicles
- I Edras

With that said, my second point is that the practice of communion as a miraculous event of bread turned to flesh and wine turned to blood would have been practiced at that time by the Apostles and later by the Apostolic Fathers because the first church to develop in Christ apart from the Roman church was the Greek church, now called Orthodox. The fact that they also kept communion a miracle which they call the **Mysterion** testifies to the body and blood belief in the early church. I love that name, **Mysterion**. The mystery behind the substantial change of bread and wine to the actual body and blood of Christ Jesus.

When Martin Luther broke away from the Catholic Church to begin Lutherans, around 1,500 years after Jesus walked the Earth, they kept the standard of bread and wine becoming the body and blood of Christ. The adjusted teaching of **Consubstantiation** was already being considered well before Luther's birth, and he seemed to consider such teachings. If I understand correctly, the Lutheran Church made Consubstantiation a canonical doctrine in their church over the next century or so after Luther's death.

When Henry the VIII began the Anglican Church so he could divorce his wife, the Bishop of Canterbury made no immediate changes to the practice of communion as the substantial body and blood of Christ.

In short, the roots of our faith in the elements of communion started with a miraculous change of substance teaching.

Don't believe me? That's fair. Like I said, I was trying to see what Scripture taught on the subject and could be seeing something in the wrong light. I don't think so, at present. It has kept me up many nights trying to sort out what Holy Scripture clearly said about Holy Communion.

What wonderful majesty! What stupendous condescension! O sublime humility! That the Lord of the whole universe, God and the Son of God, should humble Himself like this under the form of a little bread, for our salvation . . . In this world, I cannot see the Most High Son of God with my own eyes, except for His Most Holy Body and Blood.

St. Francis of Assisi

Chapter 6 – The Apostolic Fathers and Saints

With that said, what if I quoted a few of the Apostolic Fathers and early church theologians? I quote them not to equate their words with the authority of Scripture, but their writings responsibly display and testify of the beliefs practiced by the early church, taught to some of them directly by the Apostles. You likewise can do your own Google search and find many more quotes by the early church theologians regarding a transformative change of bread and wine to the Body and Blood of Christ. I will quote just a few.

St. Ignatius of Antioch

Ignatius of Antioch was one of the Apostolic Fathers; one of the men who would take the message of Christ and the gospel into the second century after all the Apostles had moved to Heaven.

Ignatius was converted by the Apostle John. He was martyred by ravenous lions in the Roman Colosseum, ordered by Emperor Hadrian. As terrible as that sounds, Ignatius often said that his life in Christ would not be complete if he did not die a martyr's death. These are the earliest non-Biblical quotes I found to share with you, written early second century. Ignatius wrote this while in captivity, being transported to Rome to face execution by lions.

Ignatius wrote: "*I am God's grain,* *and I am being ground by the teeth of wild beasts in order that I may be found [to be]* **pure bread for Christ**. *My love* *has been crucified, and there is in me no fire of material love, but rather a living water, speaking in me and saying within me, 'Come to the Father.' I take no pleasure in corruptible food or in the delights of this life. I want the* **bread of God which is the flesh of Jesus Christ,** *who is the seed of David; and for drink I want* **his Blood which is incorruptible love."**

Also, Ignatius speaking Against a Heretical Teaching:

"Consider how contrary to the mind of God are the heterodox in regard to the grace of God which has come to us. They have no regard for charity, none for the widow, the orphan, the oppressed, none for the man in prison, the hungry or the thirsty. They abstain from the Eucharist and from prayer, because they do not admit that **the Eucharist is the flesh of our Savior Jesus Christ**, *the flesh which suffered for our sins and which the Father, in His graciousness, raised from the dead."*

"Letter to the Smyrnaeans", paragraph 6. circa 80-110 A.D.

St. Justin Martyr

As his name suggests, he was beheaded with six other Christian brothers around 163-167 A.D. He wrote a whole bunch about Jesus and the early church. Regarding Communion,

Justin Martyr Wrote: *"This food we call the Eucharist, of which no one is allowed to partake except one who believes that the things we teach are*

*true and has received the washing for forgiveness of sins and for rebirth, and who lives as Christ handed down to us. For we do not receive these things as common bread or common drink; but as Jesus Christ our Savior being incarnate by God's Word took flesh and blood for our salvation, so also we have been taught that the food consecrated by the Word of prayer which comes from him, from which our flesh and blood are **nourished by transformation, is the flesh and blood of that incarnate Jesus."***

"First Apology", Ch. 66, inter A.D. 148-155.

St. Irenaeus of Lyons

St. Irenaeus of Lyons lived at the same time as Justin Martyr. He studied under Polycarp of Smyrna and wrote bunches against the heresy of Gnosticism. Polycarp was brought to Christ and directly mentored by the Apostle John. Regarding Communion,

St. Irenaeus Wrote: *[Christ] has declared the cup, a part of creation, to be **his own Blood,** from which he causes our blood to flow; and the bread, a part of creation, he has established as **his own Body**, from which he gives increase to our bodies."*

St. Irenaeus of Lyons, Against Heresies, 180 A.D.

Also:

*"So then, if the mixed cup and the manufactured bread receive the Word of God and become the Eucharist, that is to say, **the Blood and Body of Christ**, which fortify and build up the substance of our flesh, how can these people claim that the flesh is incapable of receiving God's gift of eternal life, when it is **nourished by Christ's Blood***

*and Body and is His member? As the blessed apostle says in his letter to the Ephesians, 'For we are members of His Body, of His flesh and of His bones' (Eph. 5:30). He is not talking about some kind of 'spiritual' and 'invisible' man, 'for a spirit does not have flesh and bones' (Lk. 24:39). No, he is talking of the organism possessed by a real human being, composed of flesh and nerves and bones. It is this which is nourished by **the cup which is His Blood**, and is fortified by **the bread which is His Body**. The stem of the vine takes root in the earth and eventually bears fruit, and 'the grain of wheat falls into the earth' (Jn. 12:24), dissolves, rises again, multiplied by the all-containing Spirit of God, and finally after skilled processing, is put to human use. These two then receive the Word of God and become the **Eucharist, which is the Body and Blood of Christ**."*

-"Five Books on the Unmasking and
Refutation of the Falsely

St. Clement of Rome

Clement was the third bishop of Rome. Mentored by St. Peter, he is considered the third Pope of the early Christian church founded by Christ and His Apostles.

Clement Wrote: *"The Word is everything to a child: both Father and Mother, both Instructor and Nurse. **'Eat My Flesh,' He says, 'and drink My Blood.'** The Lord supplies us with these intimate nutrients. He delivers over **His Flesh**, and pours out **His Blood**; and nothing is lacking for the growth of His children. **O incredible mystery!**"*

-"The Instructor of the Children" [1,6,41,3] ante 202
A.D.

Well, if it's just a symbol, to hell with it.
                                    Flannery O'Connor

****

If I could interject here, as I mentioned earlier there are many, many early church father quotes I have intentionally left out. It would cover another large chapter for this book to add them all in. You can do a Google search and find many, many more such quotes by the early church fathers. If you don't find any, email me and I'll send you some links.

For this book, I have above quoted from the Apostolic Fathers of the first and second century. Now, I'm jumping ahead a couple of centuries to relay that this practice was still being taught and practiced by the church leaders and their congregations.

****

St. Cyril of Jerusalem

St. Cyril of Jerusalem lived in the second half of the fourth century.

St. Cyril Wrote: *"Therefore with fullest assurance let us partake as of the **Body and Blood of Christ: for in the figure of Bread is given to thee His Body, and in the figure of Wine His Blood**; that thou **by partaking of the Body and Blood of Christ,***

62

mightest be made of the same body and the same blood with Him. For thus we come to bear Christ in us, because His Body and Blood are diffused through our members; thus it is that, according to the blessed **Peter***, (we become partaker of the divine nature.) [2 Peter 1:4]*

"Catechetical Lectures [22 (Mystagogic 4), 3]

Also:

"Approaching (Communion)…come not with your palms extended and stretched flat nor with your fingers open. But make your left hand as if a **throne** *for the right, and hollowing your palm receive the body of Christ saying after it, "Amen." Then after you have with care sanctified your eyes by the touch of the holy Body, partake…***giving heed lest you lose any particle of it (the bread)***. For should you lose any of it, it is as though you have lost a member of your own body, for tell me, if anyone gave you* **gold dust***, would you not with all precaution keep it fast, being on the guard lest you lose any of it and thus suffer loss?* **How much more cautiously then will you observe that not a crumb falls from you***, of what is* **more precious than gold and precious stones.** *Then having partaken of the* **Body of Christ***, approach also* **the cup of His blood***; not extending your hands but bending low and saying in the way of* <u>worship and reverence</u>*, "Amen," be you sanctified by partaking, also of the* **blood of Christ***."*

Catechetic
Literature 5

St. Augustine of Hippo

St. Augustine of Hippo lived to see the fifth century. I felt compelled to include him because most Christians are very familiar with his name and whether they know it or not, familiar with what he wrote. He spoke of the Body and Blood of Christ different times, but none more clearly than this:

St. Augustine Wrote: *"You ought to know what you have received, what you are going to receive, and what you ought to receive daily. That Bread which you see on the altar, having been sanctified by the word of God, **is the Body of Christ**. The chalice, or rather, what is in that chalice, having been sanctified by the word of God, **is the Blood of Christ**."*

-"Sermons", [227, 21]

I have covered quotes from the early second century to the fifth century to display the practice in the early church that the Miracle of Communion was not simply symbolic, but the firm belief that common bread and wine were changed into the actual Body and Blood of Christ.

I believe Scripture is very clear about this, but since I know many who reject this teaching in Scripture, I felt strongly and it certainly added to the evidence, that the early church shared this belief, and wrote as needed to challenge others who did not accept that belief.

Just an FYI, I understand that the Christian Church, called Catholic by this time, wrote a decisive and clear teaching on this subject in the ninth century. Later, in 1215, the church came up with the term "**Transubstantiation**" to label the elements of Communion as the miraculous change to the Body and Blood of Jesus.

But, as I was researching and writing this book, I initially came with an open mind to see what the Apostolic Fathers and others in the church wrote about the Body and Blood of Jesus as Communion. As I said earlier, their words in no way supersede nor even are equal to Holy Scripture, but their writings as testimonies are completely valid for establishing early practices of the Christian Church as taught by Christ and His Apostles.

That day that I can no longer receive
Our Lord in Holy Communion,
Our Lord Himself will come to take me.
                                    Mary Potter

Chapter 7 - The Soul

One of the most common criticisms by devout, God-fearing, Christ loving Christians who hold that the bread and wine are merely a symbolic practice of communion is that there is no physical change or appearance to the elements. Bread is still bread. Wine is still wine. Our modern scanners and other equipment display no physical change to the bread and wine. When dissected by nutritionists and others, the bread and wine still are the same as unconsecrated bread and wine.

That could be a valid consideration except for a couple of thoughts. The first is that they limit God in what He can do. If He wants to change bread and wine into His Body and Blood without changing the substance, I doubt that's all that hard for Him.

Second, under the Mosaic Law, certain bread was consecrated for the Levites to eat. No one else was allowed to eat that bread. I'm not saying the shewbread in the temple and tabernacle was the Body and Blood of Christ, but it held a special consecration without changing its substance.

The third thought that occurred to me pointed to our souls. Those very people who believe Communion is merely symbolic because the bread and wine are not physically changed would also admit they have a divine soul as part of their human life on Earth – a soul that will leave the body when they die, to live forever, whether in Heaven or Hell. Yet, there's no physical proof or instrumental measuring that the soul exists. We know it exists only because God told us it does. If they can believe in the Soul which cannot be detected or measured, how can they deny belief in a divine presence beyond mere symbolism in the Communion Bread and Wine merely because of appearances?

One of the most admirable effects of Holy Communion is to preserve the soul from sin, and to help those who fall through weakness to rise again. It is much more profitable, then, to approach this divine Sacrament with love, respect, and confidence, than to remain away through an excess of fear and scrupulosity.

St. Ignatius of Loyola

Now I've believed for quite some years that the body does not contain the soul, but the exact opposite – that the body was knitted to our souls. As I have often stated, *Everyone lives forever – they just have to decide where.* If you know you have a soul that you cannot see, cannot be measured, cannot be detected with all of our modern scientific equipment, etc., then how is it harder to believe that God's Holy Spirit can change common bread and wine into the Body and Blood of Christ without changing the physical substance of the elements?

I know of a recent discussion on this debate with an evangelical pastor – a beautiful man who loves the LORD deeply and profoundly. He has given His life to serving God, and I know few men more deserving the title of Pastor. When the subject of the elements of communion were discussed, he stated that he believed it was only the symbolic presence of Jesus in the bread and grape juice they served.

The other speaking with him retorted, "Because that is all you ask for."

When I started this study, I honestly tried to see what Scripture testified and taught about the Miracle of Holy Communion. I sincerely tried to lay aside all personal bias and teachings of my youth.

Around 1980, I heard **Dr. Walter Martin** speak about this subject on his radio program *The Bible Answer Man*. I grant that it was a radio program so he could not go into as extensive an argument than he might have elsewhere, but after hearing his arguments about Holy Communion on the air, I was far, far from convinced the elements were merely symbolic by Martin's words. Yet it was that very program back in the 1980's, that compelled me to research Scripture regarding the elements of Communion. As I said earlier, at the time I sought to set aside my childhood lessons and biases regarding Communion and Eucharist to see what Scripture really taught. I was even more diligent to do that study all over again for this book.

I urge you to pray to God about this amazing miracle. The most important factor is that we practice communion in remembrance of Jesus. It's one of the three holy sacraments Jesus practiced on Earth, (the other two are Baptism and Penance, ie Confession), and the only one He commanded us to do to remember Him.

In an ever-changing world,
The Holy Eucharist is a constant reminder
Of the great reality of God's changeless love.
St. Teresa of Avila

Closing Thought on Sacraments

The bottom line for a sacrament is meant to separate men and women into a life of service to Christ. It does not have to have a special name. God calls all of us to His service, His "Holy Orders", practiced in part through the sacraments. Coming to Christ, by default, means a commitment to live fully as a minister of the gospel of Jesus Christ and share His sacraments with others as it will engage and help and increase their holy walk with our LORD. That walk certainly included Holy Communion.

It is tradition in Ireland that you're given money for your First Communion.

Roma Downey

Conclusion

I am sure you figured out my conclusions well before this point of the book. As I mentioned in the Introduction and Such, I studied Scriptures with a brutally honest eye – a sincere desire – a totally new look to see what Scripture taught on this debate. I gave it that unbiased look in 1980, and again when composing **Tossing Mountains**. Even writing and editing this small book, I tried to keep my biases in check, yet found even more Scriptural evidence to support a Transubstantiative change in the bread and wine, miraculously changed into the body and blood of Jesus Christ.

You are welcome to tell me where I'm wrong, but all such arguments must come from Scripture – not "Common Sense" arguments which are pretty much always biased.

As I've shared these words with others over this last year or so, checking and challenging my own insights, no one has told me I was wrong to my face. On the same hand, some evangelicals still hold to the elements of Communion as being simply symbolic.

This is not a criticism. From my limited perspective, I don't think they have the same dire sense, or personal burden, to understand Scripture on this specific subject as I have carried.

I also confess, and it should be noted and no secret that I had already completed my research before composing this book, so if it seems slanted or biased, it is totally because I had already completed my Scriptural research before composing this book.

There's a part of me that argues, *"If you think it is only symbolic, why do it?"* It has no substance. It has little meaning. It's just something we do 'cuz Jesus said to do it.

I had to rein in my personal criticisms here. There are LOTS and LOTS of symbolisms I love and practice. I am blessed over and over by the symbolic teachings of our faith in Christ, including His Parables. Lots of symbolism in Christ's own words. Even my allegorical novel, **Life's Vagabondage**, is symbolic throughout.

Still, it makes sense to me, if Jesus wanted Holy Communion to be merely symbolic, it would not be given the designation "New Covenant". The elements of bread and wine would not be given greater significance, such as St. Paul wrote in I Corinthians. John, Chapter 6, became a veritable treasure trove regarding Holy Communion, where Jesus said they had to eat His flesh and blood. Some of the disciples and locals clearly were so offended by that teaching that they stopped following Christ.

I did not include the section citing different saints over the centuries in the first upload of **Tossing Mountains** to Amazon Books. It later occurred to me to check and see what the Apostolic Fathers and later Saints wrote about. As I said, I cited just a few. Check online if you'd like. You'll find literally dozens of early church saints who practiced the belief in bread and wine becoming Christ's body and blood. I cannot believe that they intentionally changed that practice to be different from what the Apostles personally told them.

Now, I'm just a regular person who loves Christ, loves reading Scripture and loves praying. I don't get everything right theologically. I am still learning. I am still on the road of growing in my faith. I pray this little part of the journey can also be a blessing to you.

God bless you, always and all ways. Dave Stoeckl, Sequim, WA USA

If the Angels could envy, they would envy us for Holy Communion.

Pope Pius X

---

* Many Thanks to you for sharing time with me and this Bible study regarding the elements of bread and wine used in the Sacrament of Holy Communion.

Your Reviews are greatly appreciated.

Feedback also always welcome.

May God's blessings be ever with you in your walk with Jesus and His Holy Spirit.

If you like the book,
please review it.
It's very helpful for letting
others know what you thought.

Other Books by David Stoeckl

- Patmos – An Apostle in Exile – A Planet on Trial (a Historic, Biblical novel)
- Patmos also available as an Audiobook
- Life's Vagabondage (an Allegorical novel)
- Life's Vagabondage Audiobook (soon coming)
- Tossing Mountains – Where are the Miracles Today Like We Read About in the Bible?
- Silhouette of God – A Bit of Poetry
- Oops! There Goes Another One (a novel)
- Julesburg Cruisin' Night (a Pictorial)
- An Awful Lot Like Me (a novella)
- Amy and Dave's Glacier Escape Tour - 2025
- Amy and Dave's Portugal Escape Tour – 2023
- Amy and Dave's COVID Escape Tour – 2021
- Your Quick Guide to Understanding Subsidized Housing (How to apply for HUD Housing)
- His Heart Art – a Devotional (pen name David Sterling
- 52 Diets a Year (pen name David Sterling)
- 40 Days Christian Devotional (Pending)

(& More To Come)

www.ingramcontent.com/pod-product-compliance
Lightning Source LLC
Chambersburg PA
CBHW032212040426
42449CB00005B/563